CENGAGE Learning

MW01074041

Poetry for Students, Volume 29

Project Editor: Ira Mark Milne Rights Acquisition and Management: Mollika Basu, Jermaine Bobbitt, Sara Teller, Robyn Young Composition: Evi Abou-El-Seoud Manufacturing: Drew Kalasky

Imaging: Lezlie Light

Product Design: Pamela A. E. Galbreath, Jennifer Wahi Content Conversion: Civie Green, Katrina Coach Product Manager: Meggin Condino © 2009 Gale, Cengage Learning

For product information and technology assistance, contact us at **Gale Customer Support, 1-800-877-4253.**

For permission to use material from this text or product, submit all requests online at **www.cengage.com/permissions.**

Further permissions questions can be emailed to **permissionrequest@cengage.com** While every effort has been made to ensure the reliability of the information presented in this publication, Gale, a part of Cengage Learning, does not guarantee the accuracy of the data contained herein. Gale accepts no payment for listing; and inclusion in the publication of any organization, agency, institution, publication, service, or individual does not imply endorsement of the editors or publisher. Errors brought to the attention of the publisher and verified to the satisfaction of the publisher will be corrected in future editions.

Gale
27500 Drake Rd.
Farmington Hills, MI, 48331-3535

ISBN-13: 978-0-7876-9893-5
ISBN-10: 0-7876-9893-8
ISSN 1094-7019

This title is also available as an e-book.

ISBN-13: 978-1-4144-3834-4
ISBN-10: 1-4144-3834-6
Contact your Gale, a part of Cengage Learning sales
representative for ordering information.

Printed in the United States of America
1 2 3 4 5 6 7 13 12 11 10 09 08

Native Guard

Natasha Trethewey 2006

Introduction

The title of Natasha Trethewey's Pulitzer Prize-winning collection *Native Guard* (2006) references a regiment of African American soldiers, some of whom were freed slaves, others of whom had enlisted with the Confederate army but had ultimately escaped the rule of white Southerners. This special regiment fought for the Union army during the Civil War, standing guard on Ship Island, off the Mississippi shore, to ensure that Confederate prisoners did not escape.

The title poem of the collection is told in the voice of one of the black soldiers, a freed slave who sees similarity between his role as a soldier and that of a slave. The work is manual labor, just like before, and the rations are also very familiar. The soldier recounts the passage of time as he records his thoughts in a journal-like poem. The poem laments the loss of life, dignity, and freedom. At one point, the poem points out that everyone is a slave to destiny.

Author Biography

Natasha Trethewey was born in Gulfport, Mississippi, in 1966 to a white father and a black mother. Her father, Eric Trethewey, a poet, and her mother, Gwendolyn Grimmette, a social worker, divorced when Trethewey was six years old. She and her mother then moved to Georgia, where her mother earned a master's degree and later remarried. Trethewey's stepfather murdered her mother several years later, in 1985. Trethewey was nineteen at the time. Trethewey's biracial identity as well as her mother's murder are topics that Trethewey often examines in her poems.

Trethewey earned her bachelor's in English from the University of Georgia; her master's in poetry from Hollins University in Roanoke, Virginia (where her father was a professor); and an MFA in poetry from the University of Massachusetts. Trethewey taught as an assistant professor of English at Auburn University in Alabama before taking on the professorial position of Phillis Wheatley Distinguished Chair of Poetry at Emory University in Decatur, Georgia.

Trethewey's work has appeared in many different publications, including *The Best American Poetry* (2000 and 2003), *Agni*, *American Poetry Review*, *Callaloo*, *Gettysburg Review*, *Kenyon Review*, *New England Review*, and the *Southern Review*. Trethewey's first collection of poems,

Domestic Work (2000), won the 2001 Mississippi Institute of Arts and Letters Book Prize and the 2001 Lillian Smith Award for Poetry. Her second collection, *Bellocq's Ophelia* (2002), received the 2003 Mississippi Institute of Arts and Letters Book Prize, was a finalist for the Academy of American Poets' James Laughlin and Lenore Marshall prizes, and was named a 2003 Notable Book by the American Library Association. Her 2006 collection, *Native Guard*, won the 2007 Pulitzer Prize for Poetry.

November 1862

Trethewey divides her poem "Native Guard" into time frames, beginning with November 1862. In the first stanza, in the voice of an African American soldier, Trethewey provides the background of this soldier, his life prior to enlisting in the army. The soldier reflects on his life as a slave. First Trethewey provides a sense of the physical landscape of a Southern plantation that sits on the side of a river. The Gulf of Mexico is mentioned, setting the scene in one of the gulf states, along the shoreline. The soldier was once a slave, but he mentions that he was already freed earlier in 1862. However, he seems to be so newly freed that he has to remind himself that he is no longer a slave.

The soldier then recounts some of his memories of having been a slave ever since being born into slavery. Marks upon his back, signs of having been whipped, are proof of his history. The soldier makes a reference to Ascension Parish, located in the southeastern part of Louisiana (which has parishes instead of counties). The soldier is thirty-three years old. He compares the marks on his back, which have recorded his history up to now, with the marks he will now make with ink on paper. This is his new form of history taking, as a power that was once the slaveholder's has become his own.

December 1862

A month has passed, and the soldier now mentions a sergeant, comparing the sergeant to a slave master. Both the sergeant and the slave master have their ways of bringing their men around to obeying orders. The soldier and his fellow mates learn to march under the sergeant's drills, but instead of being given guns, the black soldiers are told to dig ditches and work like mules, carrying supplies. The soldier suggests that the top officer over the black soldiers uses derogatory racial slurs when referring to them. In addition to having to listen to the verbal abuse, something they became accustomed to as slaves, the black soldiers are given only half as much food as their white counterparts are granted. This too, the soldier says, is a familiar slave routine. The soldier admits that in order to supplement their supplies, they steal from abandoned homes. This implies that the regiment is not yet on Ship Island, as there are no homes there. Not only do the black soldiers take food from these houses, but also this soldier found in one the paper and ink that he needed to write his journal. The journal this soldier found is already written on, so he crosses out the other person's words (suggesting that these are a white person's writings) and writes his own thoughts over them. This provides an image of the black man rewriting history or possibly just telling it from another perspective.

January 1863

Two sections of this poem have the same date, that of January 1863. In the first section, the soldier mentions a ship that has taken him to Ship Island. The name of the boat and the name of the fort on Ship Island remind the soldier of the North, where many black people live free, the destination of many runaway slaves in the South. This soldier never dared attempt to take that road to freedom, and yet, he is delivered to a place that suggests that journey, at least in name. Though the environment of Ship Island is not easy to endure, as it is too hot and the air is filled with biting insects, the soldier enjoys the open expanse of the horizons, where he can look out across the gulf and dream. On the water he sees the boats that have arrived from the North, filled with Union soldiers who have come to the South to help free the slaves. Then he ponders the question of slavery. Are he and his fellow African Americans the only ones who are slaves? Isn't everyone bound by fate? At this point in the poem, the soldier is considering the equality that everyone is born with as well as the similar patterns that everyone shares in dealing with the world and one's own destiny. He sees the potential for a positive future, a new life that promises to make him feel better as he more fully realizes that he is free.

In the second stanza of January 1863, the soldier is not so hopeful. The dawn of the previous stanza, the one that promised good fortune, is now seen as a warning of danger and trouble. Supplies that were dropped off on the beach were not put in safe storage, and the men were unaware of the possible consequences. A storm came up quickly and washed the supplies away. The supplies needed to be tied down, the soldier now realizes. This image reminds him, once again, of how tied down he had been as a slave. The next day, as the men work, they begin to sing. The rhythm of the song and the sound of their voices brings them together, making them feel as one, buoyed by a sense of community that the soldier had never felt before. A fellow soldier takes off his shirt in the heat and exposes scars on his back that everyone recognizes as the marks of a whip. The ropes that are used to tie down the supplies, the other soldier points out, make sounds similar to that of the whip. This second soldier also points out how their tents blow in the wind, threatening to take off in some wild dance. These are all reminders for the soldier that if he wants to keep something, he must learn to tether it.

February 1863

An irony opens this stanza—the fact that a group of black soldiers is now standing guard over a group of white Confederate soldiers. These white rebels would have been the masters of the black soldiers were it not for the Civil War. Though the white soldiers are prisoners, the soldier comments that they are equal in a strange way; their positions could change so quickly, one taking the other's place. The white soldiers' fight for freedom has led them to be jailed.

The white prisoners are wary of their black captors and try not to look at them. The soldier narrator, realizing that most of the white men are illiterate, senses his own power over them, as he, at least, has the power of words. The white prisoners cannot write letters home except through the skills of the black narrator, who was once their slave. They do not know whether to trust him, however. The soldier thinks that they believe he is writing more than they tell him, but they can only add their signatures, each using no more than an *X*. That is their only power when it comes to the literary process; they are in the black soldier's hands.

March 1863

The narrator details some of the passages from the letters he has written for the white prisoners. They write letters to their wives, asking them how they are doing, how their land is doing, and whether the wives were able to bring in the crop, to provide the family with enough food to last. The soldier narrator mentions that he hears the white prisoners saying more than they are actually telling him; he can read between the lines, such as when the prisoners want to send photographs home so that their wives will remember them should they never return. The prisoners remember their wives waving to them as they left home. The significance of these last images is that the soldiers were departing as if they would be gone for good. Other prisoners talk of more morbid things, like the short supply of food, the oppressive heat, and the smell of death all around them. Their own physical prowess, some of the prisoners tell their families, is failing them.

April 1863

The narrator takes up the theme of death. As the soldiers die, there is more food for the rest of them. There is also mention of a battle at Pascagoula, which is close to the southern shores of Mississippi. In this battle, the black regiment proved that they were capable of fighting. The narrator mentions that many died, and he talks about burying the dead. There is a twist to this story, however. As the black soldiers retreated to their ship, white Union soldiers (who were supposed to be on the black regiment's side) began shooting at them, killing many more. The narrator heard the white colonel in charge of the black regiment make a comment that fell short of describing the way the narrator felt at seeing this senseless killing; the colonel's words described the event as if it were trivial.

June 1863

Two months later, the memorial that was supposed to bear the dead black soldiers's names engraved in stone still does not exist. There are memorials to white soldiers, however. There is mention of another battle, this one at Port Hudson, which is located in Louisiana not far from Baton Rouge, along the Mississippi River. Around 5,000 Union soldiers and some 700 Confederate soldiers died in this battle. Black regiments were involved in this battle, but, according to the poem, the commander in charge, a General Banks, paid little attention to the black soldiers who died there. The narrator remembers them in his mind, imagining a battlefield scene where a black soldier laid unburied.

Despite the prejudice and the dismissal of the sacrifices that the black soldiers are making, more black recruits come to the island, ready to give their lives. They do this because their lives are nothing but suffering anyway. They are starving and are willing to take their chances on the battlefield. The narrator closes this stanza by repeating his earlier claim that whether prisoner or guard, whether white man or black, whether free black or slave, they all share the same lot. They all will soon face their deaths.

August 1864

The name of Francis Dumas is mentioned in the opening lines of this stanza, as the narrator was once a slave of Dumas's. This master—also a black man—was good, the narrator states. Dumas is the one who taught the narrator to read and write, and he also learned about nature from Dumas, who, in other words, helped the narrator to open his mind to other possibilities beyond labor and slavery. The narrator claims that while he lived as a slave, he focused most of his thoughts on life. But his life has drastically changed: Now that he is a free man, all he deals with is death. He buries the dead and tends to their graves, which the wind is constantly disrupting. He writes letters to the wives and families of the men who are dead, keeping the horrid details to himself, though he senses that the families crave more information. He considers that the things the families are not told are like other details about the war that will not be expressed. It is as if the narrator already knows that the black regiments, in particular, will be forgotten.

1865

Possibly a year has passed. The Civil War is either over or at least near its end. The narrator takes the time, then, to list the things that need to be said about the war and his experiences. He wants to be the voice for those things that he has been told not to say. He talks about mass killings and about the maimed. He wonders what will happen to the black soldiers who are now freed but have no homes. He mentions the dead black soldiers who were left on the battlefields to rot or to be eaten by wild animals. Soldiers missing limbs still feel them as if they were still attached, just as the soldiers who were not killed remember those who were. Missing are not just the bodies but also the memories of those soldiers, who, if they were lucky enough to be buried, do not have names on their graves. No one has time to record their stories, so who will remember them? Their bodies have now turned the battlefields green, and traces of their lives have been all but erased.

Themes

Death

The theme of death permeates Trethewey's poem. Beyond the death that symbolizes the inevitable end that everyone must eventually face, there is also the senseless death that comes from war, prejudice, and negligence. With the setting being the Civil War, one would expect the topic of death to be present, and Trethewey indeed goes far with this theme, talking about massacres and slaughter—huge losses that insinuate overkill. There are men who die on the field of battle as well as men who die of disease because they have been locked up in cells that are unfit for living. The men are cramped into spaces that are poorly ventilated, and they are poorly fed; sanitation is lacking, and the heat is sweltering and suffocating. There are also the deaths of soldiers shot by their own comrades.

A presence of psychological death can also be found in this poem. As Confederate soldiers rot away in prison, they lose hope of ever returning to their families. They write letters home and have visions of their wives while strongly sensing that they will never see them again. Hints of the death of dignity can also be found, as the black soldiers realize that their names will not be remembered because they are discounted as humans, deemed unworthy of even a body count when they fall dead in the fields.

Prejudice

Prejudice as a theme is apparent throughout the poem. The black men in the regiment might be freed slaves, but they have not escaped the prejudice that was partially responsible for their being held captive in the first place. They may have been promised freedom, but that freedom came with the price of prejudice. They soon learn that they are the cheap soldiers, the ones who receive less pay and less food than their white counterparts. They work harder, performing all the heavy labor and dirty jobs that need to be done, like tending the dead and their graves, cleaning the toilets, and digging daily wells. They are referred to in derogatory terms not only by the men they work with but also by their supervisors. They remain uncounted and forgotten after they fall. While the white soldiers come and go, stopping on Ship Island only for a few days, the black soldiers are stationed in that unhealthy place for three years. They are mistrusted not because of their deeds or their morals but because of the color of their skin. When given a chance to fight, they prove not only their worthiness but also their valor, volunteering to take the front positions, like pawns in a game of chess. When they turn around and look for cover, they are met by their own fellow Union soldiers shooting at them.

Topics for Further Study

- To give your classmates a more intimate sense of what it was like to be a slave, find a book with one or more slave narratives—stories told by slaves—and commit a passage or two to memory. Then recite the passages in front of your class, taking on the persona of the person who wrote the narrative.

- Read another black poet's work, choosing someone such as Rita Dove, Lucille Clifton, Maya Angelou, or Nikki Giovanni. Then compare that poet's work with Trethewey's. How do their voices compare or contrast? Are there similarities in the topics that they focus on? Is one poet more personal than the other? What time frames do they write about? What are the social contexts surrounding their lives and their poetry? Write a paper on your findings.

- Read about black soldiers' experiences in the Civil War. List the battles they were involved with and position those battles on a map. Find as many statistics as you can concerning the number of black soldiers in each regiment and the numbers of deaths. Also find out how many medals of honor were won. In what battles were they won? Were any black soldiers dismissed dishonorably? What role did black soldiers play in the Confederate army? Where did they fight? Place as much information as you can on your map and then use the map throughout a presentation as you explain the details that you have uncovered.

- Research the layout of Ship Island during the Civil War. Where were the prisoners kept? Where did the guards sleep and eat? What did Fort Massachusetts look like, and what was it used for? Create a three-dimensional model of the island and its fort. Make the model as realistic as possible to give your fellow students an idea of what life was like during the three years that the Native Guard lived on the island.

Captivity and Freedom

The double-sided theme of captivity and freedom is played out in the poem in different ways. The narrator of this poem tells the readers that he has spent thirty-three years of his life as a captive. When he is finally given his freedom, he realizes that his freedom is not much different than his captivity, as he is still told what to do and where to go. He still works at very difficult manual labor. He is poorly fed and has the constant fear of death hanging over his head. He might be free, but white people still hate him and treat him like he is less than human. However, he is free in his mind, as his master was an educated black man who taught him to read and write and to study nature. Yet, his body still belongs to the army. The white Confederate prisoners are also caught in this irony. Where once they were free men who had enslaved black men, now they are held captive and are at the mercy of the freed slaves. Thus, the white captives certainly feel they have reason to be wary of the black soldiers. They spent most of their lives belittling black slaves, and now they must depend on black soldiers for their lives. They have lost their freedom to choose whom they want to deal with and whom they can ignore.

Remembrance

As a person comes close to the end of his or her life, there is often a certain question: Will I be remembered? Trethewey wonders about remembrance in "Native Guard". Who will remember this regiment of black soldiers? How many history books skip over this portion of the past and others like it? Trethewey, then, takes up the cause of remembering. She wants to tell the story of the Louisiana Native Guard. Unlike the generals and colonels, she wants to count the heads, inscribe the names, bury the dead, and write about the experiences of at least one soldier who spent three years of his life helping, as best as he was allowed, to fight in the Civil War. What is a life, this poem seems to ask, if it is not remembered? As the narrator of this poem helps the white illiterate soldiers write home to their families, asking their wives and children not to forget them, Trethewey also writes home, in a way, asking her readers not to forget these men. The narrator says that he remembers his youth by the scars on his back, but now that he is thirty-three and a man, he wants to remember in a different way. So he crosses out the writing of a white man and tells a similar story but through a different perspective, a perspective that, if not written down, would never be remembered.

Style

Sonnet

"Native Guard" is written in the form of a sonnet sequence. The word *sonnet* comes from the Italian and means "little song." As a poetic form, a sonnet consists of a logical progression of several verses, with a total of fourteen lines. Traditionally, a sonnet has a rhyming scheme, however, Trethewey's sonnet sequence is unrhymed. Her poem contains ten beats to each line, clustered in two beats per foot, with five feet per line, in what is called iambic pentameter (a scheme often used by Shakespeare). The sonnet was considered an old-fashioned form in the early twentieth century, especially when free verse (which has no rhyming or standard beat) became a recognized form. Free verse, poets argued, was more like normal speech or conversation and was thus appropriate for the confessional type of poetry that was then popular. Since the turn of the twenty-first century, some poets are turning back to the sonnet form, with and without rhyming patterns. Some twentieth-century poets who helped to modernize the sonnet form are Robert Frost, Edna St. Vincent Millay, E. E. Cummings, Jorge Luis Borges, Pablo Neruda, and Seamus Heaney.

Most sonnets are divided into two parts. In the first part, the theme of the poem is provided. It is also in this first part that the poet (or speaker of the poem) raises a question. In the second part of the poem, the speaker attempts to answer that question or at least makes the point of the poem very clear. This transition between the presenting of the problem or question and the subsequent making of a point is called the turn of the sonnet. Such a turn can also be found within a broader sonnet sequence; the turn in Trethewey's sonnet sequence could likely come between the two verses that are both identified as "January 1863." From the beginning of the poem up until the first "January 1863" verse, the speaker talks about his past: what his life was like until he arrived on Ship Island. He mentions his enslavement and then his so-called freedom as a Union soldier. From the second verse called "January 1863" until the end of the poem, the speaker goes into the details of the conditions he faces as a black soldier on the island.

Repetition of Lines

Each verse of Trethewey's poem ends with a line that is then to some degree repeated in the first line of the next verse. Some of the same words or images are used in both lines, thus tying the verses together, carrying over similar themes. At the end of the first verse, she uses the image of a master and a slave and the concept of sharpening, which is again repeated in the first line of the second verse. The lines are not exact replicas of one another, but they are related. The same is true for each of the following verses. Sometimes the repeated lines are twisted slightly, using similar words but changing the images, thus providing the reader with different interpretations.

Fictional Character as Speaker

The speaker of a poem is not always the same as the voice of the poet. This is obvious in Trethewey's poem, as the fictional speaker confesses that he was once a slave and is now a soldier in the Louisiana Native Guard. Readers gain further knowledge of the speaker as the poem progresses. He is a free man now, one who can read and write. By taking on the persona of such a speaker, the poet can provide more intimate details of what it was like to be a black man on Ship Island, having to watch over the white Confederate soldiers, many of whom used to own slaves. Readers can see the conditions through the speaker's eyes, rather than reading lines that the poet could only have written through historic accounts. The fact that the speaker is literate and keeps a diary gives the poem vitality and veritableness, as if readers are looking over the man's shoulder and witnessing the writing as well as the experiences that the speaker is recording. If the poet had written from a third-person perspective, as an observer from a distance, the poem might not have been as touching or moving.

Ship Island and the Native Guard

Sitting twelve miles off the shores of Mississippi, Ship Island, a barrier island in the Gulf of Mexico, became the site of a Union army presence in the South during the Civil War. Shortly after the Union army lost the first battle of the Civil War, Major General Benjamin F. Butler was given permission to set up a volunteer army based on Ship Island. His plan was to set up a camp there, from where he and his army would then take control of Mobile, Alabama, and eventually New Orleans. Butler brought two regiments with him from the North. Other troops followed; but most of the white regiments came and went in a matter of days or weeks. In contrast, a unit of black soldiers, referred to as the Louisiana Native Guard, assembled on Ship Island and stayed there for three years.

The Native Guard arrived in 1863. The unit was made up of recent slaves and those who had been previously freed. They mostly came from Louisiana, especially the New Orleans area. When the Native Guard moved onto Ship Island, they were met with hostilities from white Union soldiers already stationed there. Noting that the tension between the two groups was counterproductive, the military leaders eventually decided to remove the white Union soldiers to other outposts, leaving the black Native Guard the only army unit there.

The prison situation on Ship Island was first set up in 1862. The prison was used for Confederate prisoners of war as well as for Union soldiers who had committed serious crimes. The number of prisoners on the island peaked in April 1865. By June of that year, all prisoners had been sent to other locations.

Life for the Native Guard soldiers was not easy on Ship Island. They had to endure stifling heat, powerful thunderstorms, mosquitoes, and a lot of blowing sand. Health issues led to the deaths of many of the soldiers, including both prisoners and guards. From among the Confederate prisoners, 153 died; from among the Union side, 232 died on the island. In all, over 180,000 African Americans fought in 163 different units during the Civil War.

At the time of the Civil War, Ship Island was one solid island. However, in 1969, Hurricane Camille, a major storm that hit the Mississippi shore, split the island in two. The islands are now called East Ship Island and West Ship Island. Today, West Ship Island is a tourist attraction. In 2005, Hurricane Katrina caused a thirty-foot wave surge that washed over the island, taking most buildings, notably except Fort Massachusetts, with it.

Compare & Contrast

- **1860s:** Civil War breaks out in the

United States between the North and the South. At stake is the abolition of slavery, the first step toward equality for blacks.

Today: While inequities still exist among the races, Barack Obama, a black senator, runs for the position of president of the United States in 2008.

- **1860s:** Small numbers of black soldiers fight in the Civil War between the states. Units composed of black soldiers are segregated from white units.

Today: Black soldiers, both men and women, fight alongside white soldiers in wars in Iraq and Afghanistan.

- **1860s:** Publications by black authors are rare. Frances "Frank" Rollin (1847-1901) writes the first biography of a freeborn African American, *Life and Public Services of Martin R. Delany*, published in 1868.

Today: Publications by black authors are prevalent. Trethewey, an African American woman, wins the Pulitzer Prize for Poetry in 2007. Other well-known contemporary black authors are Maya Angelou,

Toni   Morrison,   and   Edwidge
Danticat.

Fort Massachusetts

Fort Massachusetts, on Ship Island, provides the setting for Trethewey's poem. The fort, a sort of horseshoe-shaped structure, sits on the edge of the water on West Ship Island (formerly the western side of Ship Island). Construction of the fort began in 1859. Two years later, through the work of a hundred-man crew of masons and carpenters, the stone walls stood approximately eight feet high. That same year, Mississippi seceded from the Union, and a band of Confederate militia stormed the island and took over the incomplete fort. A short battle was fought on the island in 1861, when the Union battleship USS *Massachusetts* drew up to the island and exchanged fire with that band of Confederate soldiers, who had brought cannons to the half-built fort. Neither side declared a victory. Shortly afterward, in the middle of September, the Confederate soldiers abandoned the fort and the island completely.

By the middle of 1862 the Union occupied Ship Island and its still half-built fort, with about 18,000 troops stationed there off and on. The U.S. Army Corps of Engineers resumed the construction of the fort at this time and also erected forty other buildings that were used as hospitals, barracks, and a mess hall. The construction on the fort continued until 1866, at which time the fort remained incomplete. It has been assumed that the fort was referred to as Fort Massachusetts in honor of the first Union ship to try to take control of the island, though the name was not officially applied.

Today, Fort Massachusetts is a tourist attraction. With time and saltwater having worn away at the mortar holding the stones together, a restoration project was established in 2001. Although it was completely inundated with water during Hurricane Katrina in 2005, the fort remains a strong reminder of the past.

Major Francis E. Dumas

Major Dumas was one the highest-ranking African American soldiers to see battle in the Civil War. He was an educated man who spoke five languages, including English and French, and a rich plantation owner who had his own slaves. He freed and then enlisted one hundred of his slaves and created his own band in the Native Guard. From January to July 1863, Dumas served on Ship Island. After retiring from the military, Dumas became involved in politics in Louisiana, losing by two votes in seeking his party's nomination to run for governor in 1868.

Overview of African Americans Involved in the Civil War

It has been estimated that by the end of the

Civil War, at least 180,000 African Americans were enlisted in the Union army, representing about 10 percent of servicemen. Many of these soldiers served in artillery and infantry like their white counterparts, but the African American soldiers had to cope with the extra burden of prejudice. Their pay was considerably less than that of their white counterparts, with many black soldiers earning only half the pay of the white soldiers. And although they were trained to fight and eventually proved their courage and ability, black soldiers were often given the dirtiest of jobs to complete in camp. Statistics concerning mortalities estimate that one-third of all black soldiers who served during the Civil War lost their lives. African American soldiers were part of almost every major battle between 1863 and 1864. The most famous battle in which black troops fought was the confrontation at Fort Wagner in South Carolina on July 18, 1863. There, a black regiment volunteered to climb the walls of the fort and engage in hours of hand-to-hand combat with Confederate soldiers. Although they were eventually driven back, the black soldiers were highly commended for their bravery. Another impressive battle, one in which fourteen black soldiers received the Medal of Honor, occurred at New Market Heights, Virginia,on September 29, 1864.

Civil War

On December 20, 1860, after Abraham Lincoln was elected president of the United States and declared that the U.S. government could not endure slavery, South Carolina seceded from the Union. Within two months, the states of Mississippi, Florida, Alabama, Georgia, Louisiana, and Texas followed. A few months later, on February 9, 1861, the Confederate States of America was formed, with Jefferson Davis as its president. This act in and of itself did not mark the beginning of the Civil War; that would follow on April 12, 1861, when the Confederates fired cannons on Fort Sumter, off the shores of Charleston, South Carolina, which had previously been controlled by Union forces. Five days later, Virginia also seceded from the Union, as followed by Arkansas, Tennessee, and North Carolina. For four bloody years, battles were fought up and down the East Coast. After casualties of an estimated 360,000 Union soldiers and 258,000 Confederate soldiers, General Robert E. Lee surrendered his Confederate army to General Ulysses S. Grant on April 9, 1865. In a sign of victory for the Union, on April 10, 1865, the American flag was raised over Fort Sumter, where the war began. Lincoln was shot by John Wilkes Boothe at Ford's Theatre, in Washington, D.C., on April 14, 1865.

Critical Overview

Trethewey's collection *Native Guard* has been critically acclaimed and was awarded the 2007 Pulitzer Prize for Poetry. The collection contains poems about Trethewey's relationship with her mother (who was murdered when Trethewey was a teenager), the poet's biracial experience in Mississippi, and the racial history of Mississippi. The latter topic is explored in the collection's title poem. Donna Seaman, writing in *Booklist*, describes Trethewey's collection as "exacting and resonant." Seaman pays special attention to the title poem and comments on how harrowing some of the images contained in "Native Guard" are. She refers to Trethewey's "bayonet-sharp lyrics" and "loaded phrases and philosophical metaphors."

Ange Mlinko, writing in *Poetry* magazine, states that "Native Guard" attempts to bring together "the racial and the rational, as if to heal the old irrational wound inflicted by the state." This is a reference to the lack of a memorial to recognize the sacrifices that the Native Guard made during the Civil War. Although Mlinko applauds Trethewey's attempts to memorialize the black soldiers, she finds that Trethewey's form becomes a little "too pat" in the process.

David Wojahn, writing in the *Southern Review*, finds that "Native Guard" is "a superbly rendered group of unrhymed sonnets." The *Black Issues Book*

Review critic Kelly Norman Ellis in turn describes Trethewey as a "technically sound poet" whose sequence of verses in "Native Guard" demonstrates "a masterful weaving of sound and sense." Ellis concludes with the statement that in Trethewey's poems, "each word, each line represents syllables uttered in the mouths of those silenced by grief, pain and history."

Another reviewer who finds reasons to praise Trethewey's poetry is Darryl Lorenzo Wellington, writing for the *Washington Post.* Wellington states that the poet "has a gift for squeezing the contradictions of the South into very tightly controlled lines." Regarding the title poem and its sonnet sequence, Wellington remarks, "The graceful form conceals a gritty subject." In conclusion, the reviewer states that Trethewey still has room to improve her written voice, as the poet "may have only scratched the surface of her remarkable talent."

"What matters most in Trethewey's poem," writes the critic Carrie Shipers for the *Prairie Schooner,* "is the muscular eloquence of its first-person speaker." After lauding the poet behind that voice, Shipers states, "In lesser hands, this poem might have allowed the historical information to become a burden instead of an incentive." Trethewey, however, uses restraint, allowing the reader "to experience the speaker's consciousness rather than merely to imagine it." Shipers also finds that "the major stength of these poems is the compelling connections Trethewey makes between personal experience and cultural memory."

What Do I Read Next?

- In 2002, Trethewey published her second collection of poems, *Bellocq's Ophelia*. The collection is narrated by a light-skinned biracial woman who works as a prostitute in New Orleans prior to World War I.

- Elizabeth Alexander is a poet, playwright, and essayist. Her 2005 collection of poems *American Sublime* was a runner-up for the 2006 Pulitzer Prize. The poems in this collection cover various aspects of African American lives in the nineteenth century.

- Joyce Pettis's *African American Poets: Lives, Works, and Sources* (2002) provides readers with a quick snapshot of poets from the eighteenth century to today. Some of the poets included in this book are Maya Angelou, Paul Laurence Dunbar, Nikki Giovanni, and Jupiter Hammon. The book contains biographical as well as critical material.

- The poet Ai, who describes herself as a mix of African American, Japanese, and Native American, won the National Book Award for her collection of poems *Vice* (1999). In this collection, Ai takes on the voices of famous characters (such as Marilyn Monroe and the legendary comedian Lenny Bruce) as well as lesser-known common criminals.

- *The Classic Slave Narratives* (2002), edited by the renowned scholar Henry Louis Gates, Jr., provides readers with some of the best of the written personal accounts of slavery. Thousands of these narratives have been chronicled; Gates provides four of the most outstanding ones.

Sources

Ellis, Kelly Norman, Review of *Native Guard*, in *Black Issues Book Review*, Vol. 8, No. 2, March-April 2006, p. 19.

Heidler, David S., and Jeanne T. Heidler, eds., *Encyclopedia of the American Civil War: A Political, Social, and Military History*, Norton, 2000.

Mlinko, Ange, "More Than Meets the I," in *Poetry*, Vol. 191, No. 1, October 2007, pp. 56-72.

Seaman, Donna, Review of *Native Guard*, in *Booklist*, Vol. 102, No. 11, February 1, 2006, p. 22.

Shipers, Carrie, Review of *Native Guard*, in *Prairie Schooner*, Vol. 80, No. 4, Winter 2006, pp. 199-201.

Solomon, Debra, "Native Daughter," in *New York Times Magazine*, May 13, 2007, p. 15.

Trethewey, Natasha, "Native Guard," in *Native Guard*, Houghton Mifflin, 2006, pp. 25-30.

Wellington, Darryl Lorenzo, "My Bondage, My Freedom: In Her Third Collection, a Poet Plumbs Public and Personal Histories," in *Washington Post*, April 16, 2006, p. T4.

Wojahn, David, "History Shaping Selves: Four Poets," in *Southern Review*, Vol. 43, No. 1, Winter 2007, pp. 218-32.

Further Reading

Andrews, William, and Henry Louis Gates, Jr., eds. *Slave Narratives*, Library of America, 2000.

> This book includes ten classic slave narratives from such people as Sojourner Truth, Frederick Douglass, and Nat Turner. The material was gathered from stories told from 1772 up until the end of the Civil War.

Berlin, Ira, Joseph P. Reidy, and Leslie S. Rowland, eds., *Freedom's Soldiers: The Black Military Experience in the Civil War*, Cambridge University Press, 1998.

> The editors of this volume researched the National Archives and found letters and eyewitness accounts of black soldiers' experiences in the war. This book invites readers to share the experiences through first-person narratives.

Hollandsworth, James G., Jr., *The Louisiana Native Guards: The Black Military Experience during the Civil War*, Louisiana State University Press, 1998.

> Hollandsworth, through careful research, put together a thorough social and political history of the Native Guard regiments of the Union

army.

Rampersad, Arnold, *The Oxford Anthology of African-American Poetry*, Oxford University Press, 2006.

> The material in this collection covers a full range of thoughts and reflections about the African American experience. Some poets in this collection state that it is better to die than grow up black in America, whereas others celebrate their lives.

Ritterhouse, Jennifer, *Growing Up Jim Crow: How Black and White Southern Children Learned Race*, University of North Carolina Press, 2006.

> This book covers the period from shortly after slavery ended in the 1860s to before the Civil Rights Movement of the 1950s began. This era in the South was dominated by Jim Crow laws that were established by whites to continue the subjugation of African Americans living in the South.